THE
Archive Photographs
SERIES

HUYTON
WITH ROBY

THE
Archive Photographs
SERIES

HUYTON
WITH ROBY

Compiled by
Alison Cassidy

CHALFORD

First published 1995
Copyright © Alison Cassidy, 1995

The Chalford Publishing Company
St Mary's Mill, Chalford,
Stroud, Gloucestershire, GL6 8NX

ISBN 0 7524 0350 8

Typesetting and origination by
The Chalford Publishing Company
Printed in Great Britain by
Redwood Books, Trowbridge

The opening ceremony of Huyton Library at Westmorland Road, Huyton c.1930.

Contents

Introduction   7

Acknowledgements   8

1.   Bygone Days   9

2.   Huyton Life   23

3.   The Best Days of their Lives   39

4.   People and Events   55

5.   A Working Life   83

6.   Out with the Old   101

7.   In with the New   115

Acknowledgements

I would like to thank the following individuals who gave their kind permission for me to publish their photographs; The Rt. Hon Earl of Derby, Mrs Capper, Mr Norman Hatton, Mr Jim Hornby, Mr A.P. King, Mr T. Scragg.

Thanks are also due to the following people who have eluded my attempts to trace them and whose photographs have also been included in this publication; D. Atkinson, Mrs Bliner, Mr and Mrs Brennand, T. Cliff, Anne Francis and Mrs D. Jones.

Introduction

Huyton village dates back to a fifth century Angle settlement which was called 'Hitune', meaning 'landing place/farmstead'. It was probably a dry landing place in the marshes that covered the area at that time. Roby is a younger village, it grew from a tenth century Norse settlement called 'Rabil' meaning 'boundary farmstead/village. Both Hitune and Rabil were mentioned in the Domesday survey of 1086.

Several powerful families have controlled the area over the ages; from the 1200s, the De Lathom family were Lords of the manor, until 1380, when Huyton was inherited by the Harringtons and Roby passed to the Stanleys (the Earls of Derby), by marriage. However, in 1720, the Molyneux family of New Hall and Alt Grange became Lords of the Manor of Huyton (excluding Woolfall).

The march of progress began to affect Huyton with Roby by 1726. The establishment of the Turnpike Trust brought a road from Prescot to Liverpool through Roby, and the Toll Bar cottage was built. Another major development in the history of the area was the creation of the passenger railway from Liverpool to Manchester which began in 1830 after the successful trials of Stephenson's *Rocket* at Edge Hill. This was the world's first passenger railway. The branch railway station at Huyton opened in 1872.

The history of local government in the area begins in 1888 when Huyton and Roby came under the control of Lancashire County Council. Before that time the church wardens of the parish would have been responsible for some public duties and care of the poor.

It was after the formation of Huyton with Roby Urban District Council in 1894, that the modern history of Huyton with Roby begins. From that time until the 1930s the area was a quiet semi-rural corner of Lancashire, until

Liverpool Corporation purchased part of the Knowsley Estate from Lord Derby in 1932. This was done to create housing developments which could accommodate the population overflow from Liverpool's urban areas.

This decision was to dramatically alter both the built environment and the character of the village. The Council and private developers continued to build modern housing estates throughout the post-war years up to the 1960s.

In 1962, large scale demolition of the old village took place, and much of the charm of the area was destroyed. Sherbourne Square was built shortly after this and the Council Offices, DSS building, Police Station, Courts and Leisure Centre were all built between 1963 and 1972, to modern designs.

Lancashire County Council was abolished in 1974 and the Merseyside boroughs of Liverpool, Knowsley, St. Helens, Wirral and Sefton were created. Huyton with Roby then became a part of the Metropolitan Borough of Knowsley. The building of the M62 followed shortly after, putting Knowsley on the main transport and communication network in the north west.

Thus the history of Huyton with Roby, especially over the last century, reflects a considerable change in lifestyle for the population. Many older Huytonians will remember the days when Huyton was a small Lancashire village, before the influx of residents from Liverpool. That the environment of the village has changed tremendously is evident when comparing, through photographs, similar views taken at different dates, especially of the Derby Road area.

It is clear that Huyton, although having a truly ancient past and having been of great influence in the history of the north west as a whole, now enjoys the benefits of a modern, thriving town, although it has lost much of its original charm. Knowsley M.B.C. is striving to protect those areas of older buildings which still survive with conservation orders and is planning to renovate the appearance of the town centre in the near future.

Alison Cassidy
October 1995

One
Bygone Days

A view of Huyton village from St. Michael's Tower c.1880.

The old cottages near Huyton Cross are shown in this very early photograph taken c.1860-70. The gateway in the background leads to the cemetery. Jim Cave, a painter, is one of the figures on the right. The cottages are constructed of wattle and daub, a traditional method of housebuilding which has now all but died out. The cottage on the left also has a traditional thatched roof.

Huyton Cross from an early picture postcard. The date of the postcard is unknown, however, the costumes worn by those in it suggest the period 1910-1920.

Broadgreen Road (Roby Road) c.1900. The M62 motorway now runs along here. Roby Road is one of the longest established roads in the village and probably grew from a dirt path between the fields and houses. The Prescot to Liverpool Turnpike was created to enable Liverpool merchants to transport coal to Liverpool from mines in Prescot. In 1726 an act was passed and the turnpike road which ran through Roby was created.

The Bluebell Inn on the corner of Blue Bell Lane and Liverpool Road, taken c.1909 when King Edward visited Huyton. In about 1938 this building was demolished and a new public house built. The little girl in white is Nancy Richardson.

Blue Bell Hotel, Huyton.

The Bluebell Hotel from a postcard. Tramlines can be seen along the full length of the road. The bicycle and cart reflect an age when Huyton was untouched by the influence of modern, motorised transport, c. 1900.

The old Rose and Crown public house, Derby Road. Next to the shop on the left is the brewery. The employees of the brewery are pictured on page 85.

The Parish church is dedicated to St Michael the Archangel and was founded in the twelfth century by Robert De Lathom who granted it to Burscough Priory. The oldest part of the existing structure dates from 1647 but most of the building dates from 1663. The tower was added in the 1700s. Although the roof, nave and chancel were renewed in 1927, most of the church survives in its original condition.

An interior aspect of St Michael's Parish church, c.1880. The ornately carved chancel screen here was buried during the Reformation to prevent its destruction.

St Gabriel's parish rooms, Hall Lane, Huyton Quarry. The caretaker's lodge is on the right, the church itself is at the back of the building c.1910.

Huyton Lane, opposite the vicarage and cricket field (on the left). The house on the far right was occupied by Mr Stonier. The three gentlemen, left to right, are: Reg Wilson, Clarence Jackson and Alec Fletcher c.1927.

Derby Road before the turn of the century. Through the second archway to the left was Alfred Prescott's property. His parrot used to hang in a cage outside the door, but the police asked for it to be removed as its language was offensive! William Brennand's shop was next door and next to that Mr Turner's Butchers. The Boot/shoe shop belonged to Shem Robert Jones. In 1890 the business became a stationers. Notice the boot hanging outside c.1880.

Derby Road on 13 July 1906. Outside Dr Gorst's House. Several views of Derby Road at varying dates and from different angles can be seen throughout the seven chapters. Derby Road has been one of the most influential throughfares in the history of the village.

The Huyton with Roby Urban District Council offices can be seen on the right of this photograph of Derby Road. The Post Office is visible to the left c.1910.

An early view down Derby Road looking towards St Michael's parish church c.1910. The small boy on the left, near the hedge is William Birchall, with Edith and Jenny Gibson. Mrs Gibson, his mother, is on the right side of the road, in the distance (one foot on the road, close to the shops). The style of clothing worn by the children is typical of the period. Sailor suits were extremely fashionable. During the First World War, childrens' clothes became more functional and less decorative, out of necessity.

Looking down Derby Road towards the church, the old Rose and Crown pub is at the centre top of the picture. It was situated opposite the church entrance and had been an important inn on the Turnpike Road - it had stables, coaches and its own brewery. For most of the nineteenth and twentieth centuries the building was in use as a pub but it also had a history as an auction room, meeting house and jail for Quakers who disturbed church services. To the left was the Post Office c.1912-14.

Poplar Bank End c.1910. The perambulator in the photograph suggests that the family were better off than most. The first perambulator was invented in 1733 for the 3rd Duke of Devonshire, the design fitted with a harness, presumably to be drawn by a dog! The four wheeled push chair was not in use until the late 1800s.

Looking down Derby Road from the East. The Police Station can be seen on the right with a sergeant's house attached to it. On the left is Lord Derby's tithebarn, at this time, used as the infant's school c.1910.

Wellcroft House, Derby Road. This was owned by Thomas Davies until 1901. He lost his life in the Great War just before the Armistice. For many years, Wellcroft was a cab stand, the horses and coaches being kept under the arch until 1937. Sir Joseph Beecham's chauffeur, Mr Underwood, ran the business using the two cars Sir Joseph had left to him in his will. From 1937-67 it was the Jersey Dairy under Mr Waugh who brought the property from Lord Derby.

The junction of Huyton Hey Road and Derby Road in the 1920s. From left to right, can be seen Richardson's grocers and bakers, with a warehouse above, and stables. The ovens are still under the road. Next comes Mr Brennand's shop and the Wellcroft dairy, which was once the site of a well. To the left is the crack which was built my Mr Turner, a bricksetter. This site eventually became a large housing complex. To the extreme left was a greengrocer and a butcher. Richardson's grocers and bakers on the corner (right) can also be seen on page 88.

The Congregational Chapel at Huyton Hey Road was known as Park Hall. It was built in 1858 and an adjoining school added in 1861. When the new chapel on Victoria Road was built in 1890 the school took over Park Hall in its entirety.

Archway Road looking east. Barton's sweet shop, which is half-timbered, is visible c.1900.

Stanley Road c.1910. The area at the top of Stanley Road by Derby Terrace is the site of Huyton Cross. Originally there was a wattle and daub house on the site but this was demolished c.1880. Derby Terrace was then built and the cross placed there by Revd Ellis Ashton in an attempt to stop cockfighting, and other barbaric sports, in front of the church.

Stanley Road. The name of the road is derived from the surname of the Earls of Derby. Thomas, Lord Stanley was given the title 'Earl of Derby' in 1485 as a reward for supporting (with his brother) Henry Tudor in the Battle of Bosworth. Henry defeated Richard the Third and became Henry VII. By 1500, the Stanleys were one of the most powerful families in Lancashire owning much land including Knowsley. The Stanleys are still the Earls of Derby to this day.

Two
Huyton Life

Bluebell lane, undated, but taken before 1977.

Croft House, Archway Road. This was the home of Mr Blain, shipowner and furnisher, in the late nineteenth century.

Junction of Derby Road and Archway Road c.1955. The building with the mock Tudor frontage is 'Nook Farm'. It is dated from the 1700s but the Victorians added the front in 1885. Tom Barton and his daughter Nell ran it . A shop was operated from the front of the farm for some years.

A view of Derby Road c.1948, showing the Jersey dairy on the right.

The War Memorial to the right of this picture was donated by Mr Nesbitt of Huyton Hey House, the chairman of Prescot cables. He lost his son in the First World War. It is now situated outside the Huyton Civic Suite.

Derby Road, looking towards the station c.1930, with Grahams Road on the right.

Tarbock Road, looking towards the garage and roundabout. Left is Blacklow Hall Farm which was on the site of Connaughton's Residential Home.

Tarbock Road c.1935. A blacksmith's shop was on the right. The photograph was taken shortly after the shops were built.

Tarbock Road.

Roby Hall was built by John Williamson in 1761 while he was Mayor of Liverpool. It was on the site of the present Bowring Park and was used by the army during the Second World War after which it was demolished. Roby means boundary/farmstead and Roby village was once a Norse settlement dating from around AD 925, one of the many such settlements from here to the Lake District.

Blacklow Hall on Tarbock Road and Roby Road junction became derelict by the 1960s and in 1963 it was demolished. It was at least three hundred years old and it was renowned for the stone lions outside the front door. There was reputedly a secret underground passage which led to Huyton church.

Blacklow House, Roby Road, was the home of the Stone family until the 1960s. When the police station in Derby Road was demolished in 1967, Blacklow was used in its place until 1974 when the police station in Lathom Road opened. Blacklow then became the headquarters of the Council library division until that was demolished in 1995.

Houses in Blacklow Brow. The cottage on the right was owned by the two Miss Sugars, both actresses who died before the First World War. This cottage belonged formerly to the dairy but was later Dr Hutchinson's house. Dr Molander used it as a surgery until he retired c.1970 when the practice moved across the road.

Blacklow Brow. This was one of the more prosperous areas of the village and reflected a pleasant countrified atmosphere, affluent merchants and tradesmen built houses during the Victorian era in several locations around the village which were secluded and peaceful. In contrast with this many of the poorer residents of Huyton lived in squalor. Contrast these residencies with the slum dwellings featured on the facing page.

Hurst Park Cottages in Huyton which became part of the slum clearance scheme in the 1930s.

The view from Ellis's Bakehouse yard in 1934, at the back of Derby Road. Going down the steps in the centre was the bakehouse. To the right was the old infant's school and to the left, on the opposite side of the road, was the police station. On this site now is the Asda Dales supermarket.

Watkin's Cottages. These were situated between Derby Road and Westmorland Road. The photograph also shows the passage by Read's shop off Derby Road (behind Irwin's shop) and looks into numbers 3 and 5 Westmorland Road, 1933.

This photograph of Watkin's Cottages was taken by HUDC as evidence for slum clearance areas 1-4 in a public enquiry held on 17 October 1933.

Townsfield Cottages in Huyton Quarry, 1933. The standard of living was very low in this area which became a slum clearance priority in the 1930s. It was one of the most squalid areas of Huyton. Townsfield cottages had a nickname "The Blue Yard" as some of the occupants packed or manufactured dolly-blue (a whitener). There were twenty two houses which shared three taps, three middens and outside toilets. Other residents worked in the mines, wire works, and brickworks.

Private enterprise houses were built on the Kingsway estate and were let in 1936.

Rupert Road, formerly Damhouse Lane. The field on the left was often flooded. To the right is Stanley Road. Professor Sam 'Putty' Grace lived in the first house on the right. William Brennand built the house by the lamp post. The school spire can be seen in the distance on the right.

A pre-1939 photograph of the old HUDC Council Offices in Derby Road shows the building before it suffered war damage. The urban district of Huyton with Roby was established on 1 January 1895. It took over the responsibility from the church wardens of the parish. Built in 1890, the offices were on the site now occupied by W.H. Smith's shop on Derby Road.

Wheathill House, Roby, shortly before its demolition. This was the home of Mr G. Pilkington and his family from 1885 until 1940. After Mrs Pilkington's death the house remained unoccupied until the Second World War when it became a P.O.W. camp for Italian prisoners and a British bomb disposal unit. After the war it became a farm and the ground floor housed poultry. It was demolished in the mid-1960s.

The wheelwright's house on the left was formerly thatched, 1960s.

Huyton Hey Manor Farm.

Huyton Hey was the home and farm of Lady Carr Saunders, born Teresa Molyneux Seel on 6 October 1895, to Edmund Molyneux Seel of Huyton and Clare Weld Blundell of Ince Blundell Hall. After her father died, Teresa and her two sisters ran the farm. In 1929 Teresa met and married Alexander Carr Saunders and moved away to raise her children. She returned as a widow in 1966 and spent her later life in charity work. She died on 12 September 1989.

McGoldrick Park and St Agnes' Road, December 1977. There were several parks in the area; recreation grounds off Derby Road and a playground in Fincham. In 1938 an area around St Bartholemews was named Page Moss Park. Jubilee Park, between Twig Lane and Dinas Lane, was approved in 1937. It had a pavillion, bowling green, and cricket and football fields.

Archway Road c. 1950.

Nutgrove Villa at the junction of Poplar Bank and Derby Road. This has been a council building for several years, 1995.

Three
The Best Days of Their Lives

St Michael's Church of England School for seven to fourteen-year-olds. The junior school was built in 1868 in Dam House Lane (now Rupert Road) to take 8-13 year olds from the infants school. The 4,800 yard site was conveyed by the Rt Hon Edward Earl of Derby under the school sites act. It was completely demolished in 1963 and another school erected on the site c. 1912.

Class photograph c.1912, from the Huyton infants school. Percy Brennand is on the back row, second from left. He grew up to run his own shop on Derby Road which sold wallpaper and paint. The children appear to be six or seven years of age and judging by their sombre expressions were under the watchful eye of the school master when the shot was taken! The school building appears on page 19.

Derby Road and St Michael's Infants School c.1960. The water fountain on the wall of the school is a well remembered feature of this part of Derby Road.

Class photograph of Huyton Congregational School (Park Hall). The clothes of the pupils date the photograph at 1910-1915.

Huyton Girl Guide troop carrying their union flag through the village c.1950.

St Michael's Church of England School for 8-13 year olds, built in 1868 and demolished in 1963. The girls entrance was to the right.

Huyton Infants School, Derby Road. Percy Brennard is in the front on the far right c.1907.

Huyton College waiting to greet Her Majesty The Queen and The Duke of Edinburgh on their visit to Knowsley, 1954.

St Michael's C of E School, class of 1956-57, B Stream. Top, left to right: Mr Firth, Margaret Butterworth, Gillian Davies, Phillip Morgan, Kayle Dury, -?-, Michael Towle, Heather ? , Mr Wardle. Second row: Rosalind Shaw, Victor Holis, Robert Sandford, Rosemary Hudson, -?- , Andrew Buckle, Christopher Smart, Andy ?, John Birchall, Ronald Wallis. Third row: Geoff Clayton, -?- , Geof Makinson, Barry ? , Joyce Ashenford, Barbara Lyon, Willie Greenhalgh, John Brindley, -?-, -?-. Front row: Eric Peacock, Olga Pickering, Alfie Owen.

Pupils in their school uniform at Huyton College c. 1915.

Lord Cozens Hardy, Miss Potts (Headmistress, 1935-58), Miss Murphy, John Stone.

A view of houses in the Orchard, a Victorian villa estate. 1977.

St Helena's House at Huyton College, 1958. The house was bought from the Stone family who moved up the road to Blacklow. It was a boarding house until the early 1900s.

Huyton Hall is the building in front and Fernwood behind. They were probably joined in 1898. The classroom was built between 1927-32. The hall was owned by Frederick Chapple for a few years prior to it being used by Huyton College.

St Catherine's, Huyton College, 1954.

Girls at work in Huyton College c.1954.

Huyton College, St Catherine's (Beaconsfield). The Revd S. Eccles lived there in the 1890s when the school was founded. The school opened on 29 January 1894 under the supervision of Miss Georgina Tarleton-Young and Miss Gertrude Anthony, after a group of Huyton residents asked the council of Liverpool College to open a girl's school in Huyton. Huyton Hall on the Orchard Estate was the original site of the school which had fifteen girls and one boy pupil when it opened.

This school group photograph of pupils from St Agnes School was taken around 1914. St Agnes' was the Roman Catholic school in the village and the children would have been given religious instruction and learned Catechism by rote. There is evidence in the classroom of the pupils work, the blackboard to the right of the door has writing about Nazareth on it - perhaps the lesson of the day. What appears to be an old fashioned gas lamp lights the room. The emphasis was on discipline and obedience in those days and the notice to the left of the door may be a list of rules.

Park Hall School c.1906. Although similar in style to the previous photograph the atmosphere in this classroom looks happier.

Huyton Park Hall and Schools.

A view of the east end of Derby Road from a postcard of c.1930. Park Hall was situated at the corner of Derby and Huyton Hey Roads.

Opposite: This unidentified young man wears the old style boy scout uniform with its distinctive hat and short trousers. This photograph was found among papers and photographs deposited in the library by an old Huytonian.

The original home of Huyton College was Huyton Hall, in an area of middle class villas known as the Orchard. The houses in the Orchard date from the 1850s. Huyton Hall and Greenhills were the first to be built between 1854 and 1861. Merchants and gentlemen enjoyed the seclusion of the Orchard as the houses were set within their own grounds. Shown here is the exterior of Huyton College.

Four
People and Events

Baker Street, Huyton Quarry, part of the slum clearance programme, clearance area one to five,
30 May 1934.

A later photograph of the old Council offices, c.1955, showing the war memorial. The Mayfair cinema can be seen to the right which was opened in September 1937 by Cllr J. Strathdene, chairman of H.U.D.C.. The feeling at the time was that the cinema changed Derby Road into a miniature high street. It had a seating capacity of 1,000. The cinema closed in 1960 and the building is now occupied by Boots the chemist.

Huyton War Memorial. This was given to the people of Huyton by Mr Nesbitt in memory of his son who was killed in World War One. It has moved locations several times.

On 20 December 1940, a 105 HE bomb fell on Jeffrey's Crescent, Huyton. Number 33, here, was demolished by the bomb which landed immediately outside the front of the house.

Bomb damage to 41-43 Coronation Drive. A 500 pound HE bomb made a direct hit on these properties during the May blitz of 1941.

Huyton's first council house, 27 February, 1947. Mr Loftus is seen here presenting the key to the chairman of the council. Councillors Horrigan J.P., and Crossart look on. Second left, back, is Mr Edmondson, Clerks Dept.

The railway station at Huyton taken around 1860. The station building to the left is still standing. The locomotive is believed to be an Allan 2-4-0 built between 1845-58. The station is on the oldest passenger line in the world, the Liverpool to Manchester railway which opened in 1830.

Roby Road looking towards Huyton. The tram terminus for the 6A is at the junction with Rimmer Avenue, Bowring Park Avenue and Roby Road. The tram is seen coming out of Bowring Park at the beginning of its return journey to Liverpool, October 1948.

The last tram to run in Liverpool, in Rimmer Avenue and Bowring Park Avenue, 1957.

Liverpool Road and the Bluebell Inn c. 1900.

The cellar of the old Rose and Crown Inn, 25 November 1937. It closed in 1938 and was demolished in 1967. An old gravestone was used in the cellar to stand barrels of ale on. The tombstone reads; 'Here lyes the bodyes of William Webster and Thomas his son. William who departed this life, November the third, 1686.'

The Bluebell Public House with a tram outside photographed between 1910-18. The tram is on its way to Knotty Ash from St Helens.

The return of the annual procession after the service at St Michael's in the 1930s.

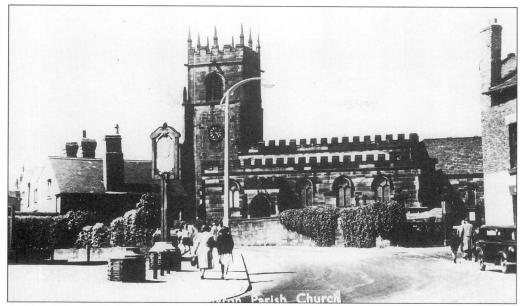

St Michael's Parish Church, c.1950. The photograph reveals an architectural error; when the roof was replaced in 1927 it should have been flat. The old cottages in Bluebell Lane can be seen behind the Inn sign on the left.

After the annual service at St Michael's church, a procession would make its way back through the village to St Gabriel's, early 1930s.

The Catholic presbytery, St Agnes, from an undated postcard.

When the Congregational Church known as Park Hall on Huyton Hey Road was taken over by the school, a new church, pictured here, was built on the junction of Victoria Road and Seel Road and opened in 1890.

Huyton Congregational
Sunday School in Derby Road
with S.B. Jones and Revd B.
Theobald leading, c.1933.

St Agnes R.C. Church, front
entrance. The parish was
founded in 1856 and the
church was built on land
owned by the Molyneux-Seel
family, close to Hey Manor.

An interior view of St Agnes, from an undated postcard, showing the altar.

St. Aloysius Church, Twig Lane, Roby. It was founded in 1934 and was to have been consecrated on 10 September 1939 but the war delayed it until 23 April 1952.

Park Hall, Huyton Hey Road. The photograph shows Lizzy Pinnington on her milk cart in the 1950s. Huyton church is in the photograph in the left foreground.

St Bartholemew's Church, Roby, built in 1868.

St Michael's Parish Church, 13 July 1905. The visit of King Edward VII who was travelling to Manchester after visiting Knowsley Hall.

A nocturnal view of St Michael's from an undated postcard.

The visit of King Edward VII and Queen Alexandra to Huyton, 6 July 1909. The Royal Party can be seen entering Huyton down Bluebell Lane.

Royal visit to Knowsley, 6 July 1909. The Royal entourage proceeds through Huyton village.

Royal visit to Huyton of King Edward VII and Queen Alexandra, 6 July 1909. The Royal procession passes along Derby Road.

Lord Derby receives King George VI with Queen Elizabeth at Huyton railway station c.1937-39.

Flower shop c.1910 and Mr Leach's old House, Derby Road.

The visit to Huyton of King Edward VII in 1909, where he viewed 30,000 troops in Knowsley Park. This photograph shows Derby Road.

King George V being received by Lord Derby at Huyton station. The King was visiting
Liverpool to open the choir and transept of the Anglican Cathedral in 1924. The locomotive is
King George I (class LNWR Roebuck No 1614) built in 1911.

The opening of the Alamein TA Centre in Huyton, 7 October 1956.

Derby Road and the visit of Her Royal Highness The Duchess of Kent, 22 July 1958. The Duchess made a tour of the Huntley and Palmer's factory during her visit.

Portrait of Thomas Beecham (1820-1907), who was the grandfather of Sir Thomas Beecham, the conductor.

The pavilion, Huyton Cricket Club, probably photographed in the 1950s.

Huyton Congregational Church AFC, 1929. There were several football teams in Huyton, including, Huyton Farm Football Club and Dovecot and Huyton Boys Club. These all benefitted from the decision of the Council in the 1920s and 1930s to provide recreation grounds for the community.

Ewanville, the home of the Beecham family from 1885, c.1930. The house was built around 1840 and was demolished c.1933. Sir Joseph built the conservatory on the right. The estate encompassed today's Blacklow Brow, The Rooley and Tarbock Road. Sir Thomas's brother Henry (known as 'Mad Harry' because of his driving activities) left it in 1928 but refused to sell until William Oldham, his head gardener died in 1932. Mr Seeley of Huyton then bought the estate and developed it.

Ewanville, a photograph of Grace Oldham, (left) with her daughter-in-law Gertrude (née Halliburton) who was the wife of Frank (kneeling) taken at the side of the gardener's cottage, near the junction of The Rooley and Roby Road.

William Oldham, head gardener, can be seen walking up the path to the house. The path ran parallel to The Rooley on the left and on the right, at the bottom, was the vinery. Off the picture to the right of the vinery were peaches, nectarines and a storehouse. The gardener's cottage was on the left at the bottom of the path.

Sir Thomas Beecham (1879-1961) as a child.

Sir Thomas Beecham's parents, Sir Joseph and Lady Josephine Beecham, née Burnett. The portrait is believed to have been taken on their engagement.

Frank Oldham (1887-1959), the eldest son of William Oldham, the head gardener with his eldest daughter Grace in the kitchen garden at Ewanville, 1926.

Sir Thomas Beecham at either St Helen's or Huyton Railway station, c.1915.

Sir Joseph Beecham (1848-1916) reproduced from a ceramics portrait.

Five
A Working Life

W. Mason, blacksmith, in front of his premises, Tarbock Road.

Mason's smithy, Tarbock Road.

Wellcroft farm in Derby Road which later became the Jersey Dairy. The policeman leaning over the gate is believed to be one known as 'Black Bernie', c.1900.

Barker's brewery, c.1914-18. This was the site of the Rose and Crown (further back) which closed in the 1930s. In the picture are, left to right: Charlie Webster, Mr Harrison, Tom Spann, Mr Philpott, Fred Spann.

The old Police Station in Derby Road was in use from 1912-67.

Westminster Bank, Derby Road, c.1930. This was previously known as Parr's Bank. Barty Evans, a relation of Sir Richard Evans, was the manager. Westminster Bank took it over around 1920. The lead sign was made by Mr Brennand.

Gore's blacksmith and wheelwright's shop at the crossroads of Blacklow Brow, Tarbock Road and Roby Road.

At the corner of Derby Road (to the left) and Huyton Hey Road were old shops, shown here in 1963. By 1977 the Midland Bank had been built on the site but was demolished in the early 1990s to be replaced by two new retail units, next to the old Central Library. 'Motorworld' now occupies one of these units.

Richardson's grocers and bakers shop c.1900 (see p.20). The shop on the corner of Huyton Hey Road sold all kinds of bread, which was baked on the premises, also corn, flour, butter and meats such as bacon and ham. Mr Richardson was German and his true name Reichardt. Because of anti-German feeling during the First World War, he anglicised his surname to Richardson.

A boot and shoe shop near the corner of Derby Road and Westmorland Road. Shem Robert Jones stands outside his cottage which was called Ty Cyhaes.

A newspaper shop owned by the grandfather of Mr S.R. Jones, where Eastman's butchers shop was until about 1923. It was knocked down in 1978 for redevelopment. 'Iceland' and the Post Office are now on this spot. The stairs to the right led to 'The Crack' where Watkins Cottages stood, c.1920.

An unusual photograph which unfortunately we do not have a good account of. These Huyton firemen were photographed in the late 1940s or early 1950s demonstrating a hand-pumped appliance of a very early type and yet the machine does not appear to be an old example. Perhaps an old Huytonian fireman can remember the event and tell us what was going on.

Derby Road from the junction of Hall Lane, Archway Road and Bluebell Lane. The house on the right was the butchers shop owned by Mr Brown who is seen here with his wife. Customers were served through the open window. The house itself was demolished in the mid-1880s. The photograph was probably taken shortly before the demolition.

Mason's shop, Derby Road in the early to mid-1930s.

The top of Wood Lane at Huyton Quarry, 1934. Fairclough's bakery can be seen where the Cocoa sign is on the far left. The other buildings are the backs of houses facing the railway.

Originally Jones's Newsagents and Tobacconists, this shop became Barlow's newsagents around 1914. The shop next door, to the left, later became a shoe shop run by Mrs Caldwell. During the Second World War the shop was responsible for distributing clothing and food coupons.

St John's Civil nursing reserve, during the Second World War, c.1940. Dr Molander is on the right and on the back row, fourth from the right, is Mrs Brennand.

Mr Mason's Shop, in the 1930s.

Mr and Mrs Mason.

94

William Brennand, born 6 February 1843, died 1918. He was a plumber, decorator and contractor on Derby Road.

Brennand's painters and decorators was established in 1810 in Rupert Road (then called Dam House Lane). In 1853 the business moved to Derby Road and in 1950 Mrs P. Brennand started the wallpaper and paint business.

Shown here are Mr and Mrs Brennand in their shop in 1953.

A view of Derby Road looking in the direction of St Michael's church (not visible), c.1910. At the far end is the old Rose and Crown which was not used as a pub after 1938. A row of shops is visible with Jack Birchall's petrol pumps in the foreground.

This photograph shows the junction of Huyton Hey Road and Derby Road in the 1960s. The present post office is on the site of the second building on the right which was demolished. Before this, the single storey building in the centre was the temporary post office which later became an office. At the time the photograph was taken the telephone exchange was under construction behind it. The latter was demolished in 1994.

The junction of Derby Road and Huyton Hey Road in the 1960s.

Derby Road in 1975. From left to right can be seen the Midland Bank, the Rose and Crown, the church and Victorian buildings on the Lathom Roadside. Next to the electricity shop was the bicycle shop. Part of Sherbourne Square shopping precinct, can also be seen to the right.

Sherbourne Square in Huyton was built in about 1962. The archway through the centre (right of the trees) leads through to Derby Road. Hardy's in this picture is now 'Supasnaps'. The Chinese Restaurant is now a hairdressers.

The most popular greengrocers shop in 1977 was at 23 Derby Road. Queues of this size were a regular occurrance.

Another view of the shops on Derby Road (opposite the Midland bank). The DHSS and Department of Employment building can be seen to the left . This photograph was taken on 5 February 1975.

Derby Road in 1975. Alongside the Victorian building on the Lathom Road side can be seen the cycle shop. These buildings were later demolished to make way for 'ASDA'.

Six
Out with the Old

Huyton Quarry near the present industrial estate was a small area of nineteenth-century terraced housing where workers of the local farming and coal mining industries dwelled. Much of the area was demolished in the 1930s as part of a huge slum clearance programme. This is Elm Street, c.1960.

Another street in Huyton Quarry, this time Derby Street, showing once more small terraces. This is the only area of Huyton where such houses are still to be found. Built to the east of the boundary fault on middle coal measures, this area had a reputation for being overcrowded. c.1955.

This view from Derby Street to Hall Lane shows the Seel Arms public house (left) c.1955.

The Longview Estate was developed by Liverpool Corporation under a 1930 Act of Parliament and became a densely populated area. Most of Huyton's housing growth was brought about to accommodate population overspill from Liverpool. During the postwar period the demand for housing was at its greatest and this was Huyton's most rapid time of growth.

The Longview Estate from Knowsley Heights at the junction of Bluebell Lane and Liverpool Road, c.1960.

Detached houses in St Mary's Road, c.1968.

Liverpool Corporation made provisions for shopping facilities at each of its housing developments. These shops were built in 1950 in Bakers Green Road alongside the development of Bakers Green Estate.

The 'Huyton Farm' Estate was the first built by Liverpool Corporation within the Huyton boundary. Council houses on Woolfall Crescent are shown here. These tenants would have paid combined rent and rates to Liverpool Corporation who would have then refunded the rates to Huyton with Roby Urban District Council.

Eight, ten storey tower blocks were constructed by Liverpool Corporation at three sites; Woolfall Heath Avenue, Primrose Drive and Bluebell Lane. The flats shown here are at the junction of Bluebell Lane and Liverpool Road.

A three storey block of flats on the St John's Estate, Browning Close. Like many others it was built at a time when Huyton with Roby District Council needed to maximize use of the available space for house building

Houses at St Anne's Road on the St John's Estate would accommodate one family on the ground floor and another on the top floor, for which there was a separate entrance. This was part of a scheme to provide a variety of different types of housing for Huyton.

Shops were an important focal point for the community life of each estate, even the privately developed estates had these facilities. Acacia Avenue is shown here, a part of the Wheathill Paramount Estate.

As the St John's Estate was half a mile from the shopping centre at Huyton village these shops would have served the whole of the community on a day to day basis and been an important resource for the community.

Prefabricated bungalows in Windsor Road, off Western Avenue. These temporary brick and concrete constructions were a short term solution to the housing problem and many were demolished by the early 1970s.

Western Avenue. These houses were built on a site which was cleared of prefabricated bungalows in 1967-68. By this time the shortage of housing was becoming a serious problem. In 1965, projected population estimates indicated that by 1971 the urban district would be 8,200 units short and would not be able to meet the demand. In response, negotiations were made to purchase land in the rural district of Whiston to create an overspill estate between Lickers Lane and Cumber Lane.

Council housing in Darwick Drive, built on the St John's Estate in 1948.

Pluckington Road and Merton Close on the Pluckington Estate which was situated on the eastern fringe of the urban district when it was built in the late 1960s.

One of the oldest firms on the industrial estate was the Tushingham Metallic Brick Company, established in 1927. It opened its brickworks on Ellis Ashton Street in 1949. Unlike the other manufacturing, retailing and warehouse industries on the estate, it relied on local supplies of boulder clay and coal measure shale to operate. The view from Wilson Road shows the kilns which were in use. The tall cement silo on the left belonged to Ready Mixed Ltd., c.1968.

The Tushingham Metallic Brick Company open-cast shale workings at the Whiston site. The firm moved to Whiston in 1899 and set up the Huyton works in 1927 (Ellis Ashton Street). Shale and boulder clay drawn from local sources were made into bricks.

The Tushingham Metallic Brick Company. A lorry can be seen delivering shale to the preparation shed. Raw materials were mined at both Huyton and Whiston and firing also took place at both sites.

The Tushingham Metallic Brick Company. This photograph shows the chimney, preparation sheds (left) and kilns (right). The company name derives from the shale used in the production of the bricks - shale was often referred to locally as 'metal'.

After the process of firing, the bricks were taken from the kilns and put into stock piles.

The Wheathill Estate was built on what was the fringe of an area of green belt, in the late 1960s. This is Oak Road. Both the estate and the green belt area, which stretched as far as the Netherley Estate, can be seen.

Derby Road, Huyton, during the town centre redevelopment and before the clearance of the site to the left which became WH Smith and Sons. On the right, near the 'no left turn' sign, are the remains of the Huyton dairy.

Sherbourne Square houses twenty seven shop premises complete with storage facilities. The old Council offices were near this area.

Derby Road c.1970. This photograph shows the road prior to pedestrianisation. It is evident that parking was a problem along this busy shopping street. Tesco can be seen on the site which is now Kwik Save.

Westminster Bank and Midland Bank on Derby Road, c.1968. The Midland Bank is now the site of two shop units, Motorworld and the other, at the time of writing, is empty. Buildings to the right of the Midland Bank became the site of the Central Library from 1978-95. This will soon be redeveloped by ASDA Ltd. At the time the photograph was taken there were five banks in the village.

Seven

In with the New

St Michael's church photographed from the top of the Council Offices in 1974. In the foreground is the Rose and Crown and through the trees on the right can be seen the vicarage. Founded in the twelfth century, the church retains some original features. It has some striking architectural points including a fifteenth-century carved screen which displays the arms of the Harrington family, some fine stained glass clerestory windows and a fifteenth century octagonal font.

The view from St Michael's Tower showing the junction of Bluebell lane, Derby Road, Huyton Lane (left) and Archway Road (right). The old Rose and Crown building can be seen on the corner of Derby Road and Huyton Lane. Further along on the left is the infants' school and on the corner of the Derby and Archway Roads is the old police station, c.1963. An earlier view from the same angle can be seen on p.9.

The junction of Westmorland Road and Derby Road. On the right was the dairy (Wellcroft Farm). To the left was a block of shops known as the Mayfair c.1950.

Looking from St Michael's church down Derby Road towards Westmorland Road. The junction of Archway Road is in the foreground, c.1950.

Tarbock Road. Part of this site is now the roundabout at the junction of Tarbock, Archway and Roby Road, c.1950.

Nook Farm. The drinking fountain on the right bears the date 1858.

The telephone exchange in the process of construction at the top end of Derby Road. A dentist called Mr Schultz had a big house on this site, c.1960.

The cross on the green at the junction of Derby Terrace, Stanley Road and Bluebell Lane. It stands close to St Michael's church on an area which was once used for cockfighting. The cross dates from 1897 and replaced a similar design of 1820, c.1960.

A view of Bowring Park, Liverpool Lodge, opposite Pilch Lane East. On the right the top of the railway bridge can be seen, 5 February 1975.

Church Road viewed from St Michael's church. The foreground at the bottom right is now a car park (Lathom Road). The middle area is now the site of the CVS centre, Clinic and Magistrates Court. In the background, the spire of the congregational church can be seen, c.1963.

Roby Road looking from Toll Bar Cottage towards Liverpool. in the early 1960s.

Established as a Norse settlement in AD 925, Roby was granted a Royal Charter by King Edward I in 1304, but competed unsuccessfully against the Prescot Fair, which was along the Liverpool to Warrington Road. By the thirteenth century, Roby was, along with Huyton, in the possession of the De Lathom family. By 1380 it had passed into the ownership of the Stanley family through marriage.

Roby Cross, 'The Boundary Stone'. This originally stood at the entrance to Lawton Road but when the latter was widened it was moved to this site. Although known as the Boundary Stone its original purpose is unknown and is perhaps the remains of an old cross. The old stocks once stood next to the stone. Edenhurst cottages, which were demolished during the road widening, can be seen in the distance.

Close up view of Roby Cross in Roby Road between Lawton Road and Carr Lane.

The Bluebell Lane end of Archway Road, 19 June 1975.

The Bluebell cottages on Bluebell Lane. These are opposite the churchyard of St Michael's and are on the schedule of listed buildings for the borough.

A good view of Derby Terrace taken from St Michael's churchyard across from Bluebell Lane in 1977.

Toll Barr Cottage at the junction of Station Road and Roby Road. At the bottom of Station Road is Roby railway station. The spire of St Bartholemew's church can be seen in the background.

Pinnington Place, 1978.

Site of the old Central Library in Derby Road before completion, c.1975.

The Huyton County Library at Westmorland Road. This was closed in 1978 when the new Central Library was completed but re-opened in September 1995 as a temporary home for the library alongside which a new library building is currently being built.

The old Page Moss branch library which was demolished in 1994. A new branch library reopened simultaneously in Stockbridge Lane.

Harold Wilson, Huyton's longstanding MP, c.1950. This photograph was taken early in his career as MP for Huyton.

Harold Wilson in Huyton town centre during the general election campaign in 1979. To his right is Cllr Seth Powell, 18 April 1979. Born in 1916, Harold Wilson was Prime Minister 1964-70 and 1974-76 and MP for Huyton from 1950 until 1976. He was knighted in 1976, on his retirement, and received a peerage in 1983. Lord Wilson died after a long illness in 1995.

An aerial photograph of Huyton with Roby. In the top right of the view is Jubilee Park. Charnwood Road is on the right of the picture. Western Avenue runs off in the foreground. The flat roofed houses have since been demolished and new estate built on the site. The building in the foreground on Western Avenue is the Dovecot Hotel, in the top left corner is the Eagle and Child in Page Moss.